Buddham Sharanam

Third Edition

Written by
Supriya Sharma

PUBLISHERS

Buddham Sharanam
Third Edition

ISBN: 978-81-949455-2-9

3rd Edition Published in 2022 by
Mage Orange Publishers
An imprint of Mage Orange Publication & Technologies
1st Floor, Reena Apartment, Kamakhya Nagar,
Adabari Tinali, Guwahati-781 012, Assam (India)
Phone : +91 7086-521-682,
Email : info@mageorange.com | info.mageorange@gmail.com
www.mageorange.org

2nd Edition

This book is based on the original manuscript by the writer without any editing.

- *The Publisher*

Acknowledgement

It is my family to whom I shall forever be grateful for their continued support in my endeavours and for having stood by me no matter the phase I went through.

Each person I met along the journey of liberation has contributed to shaping my perspective and polishing my life skills, which I think has a fantastic role in multi-dimensionalising the process.

Special thanks to the torchbearers in the fraternity of spirituality for their books, interviews, and blogs which decoded the naturalistic aspect of this religion and simplified the Buddhist teachings for me in a scientific manner, that was promulgated two millennia ago.

Preface

The Buddhist corpus is principally an expression of the Delphic dictum 'Know Thyself' and the injunction that cathartic spiritual paths throughout time and space have demanded as the vital component in authentic happiness. It is essentially about self-knowledge – who you are, how you make decisions, what drives your thoughts and actions, your relationships with others, and with the world in general. Likewise, the modern discipline of psychology, under the fatherhood of Wilhelm Wundt, churns models of behaviour and associated mental processes grafted on the theory of evolution.

It is captivating to note that first Galileo blasted the belief that the Earth was at the centre of the universe, then Darwin smashed the idea that humans were uniquely positioned at the centre of life, and now the 'self' itself is finally to be disabused of its presumption to centrality. This is when the parallelism and multiple overlaps between Buddhism and the modern discipline of psychology have become more germane to objectively focus on circumstantial human behaviour, the source of unhappiness, and ways to eliminate suffering.

Even the Dalai Lama has emphasized the compatibility of Buddhism with science and has encouraged scholars globally to conduct a critical examination of both the meditative practice and the Buddhist ideas about the human mind. Applying the Buddhist prescription requires absolute diligence, discernment, and perseverance as we encounter the resistances and capacitances from our conditioning. Does this make notable sense considering the psychology behind the evolutionary wheels? Would neuroscientists' validation of meditation undermine or enhance the spiritual significance attributed to it? How shall we design and live our lives to make us happier and felicitous people? These are some questions that motivate scientists and philosophers to dig deeper into the subject.

What provoked me personally, to explore the tenets of Buddhism and position them against the psychological mirror when spirituality wasn't my area of interest, that too in my twenties? Sometimes you meet certain people and your persona changes forever, whether you call it their influence or your nervy response to the interactions that follow. It happened with me as well in a manner I had least expected. My confidence knew no bar at that time, it used to be on cloud nine for I thought I knew myself inside out and was an unrelenting master of my feelings and actions, yet I found myself in a novel terrain whose familiarity was unfamiliar, and it didn't allow me to showcase my warrior skills.

I was sinking day by day while I attempted to lift myself against gravity. But you know, every question comes with an answer key. It's for you to unlock it. The cause whose effect landed me there was as well the cause for me to begin grazing the green pastures of Buddhism and study my behaviour in its shadow. After months and years of successful and partly unsuccessful trials of solving the puzzle, I started writing this book on the auspicious day of Buddha Purnima (full moon day commemorating the birth of Gautama Buddha) and with each passing page, gained a deeper understanding of self as to why I think the way I think or why I feel the way I feel by seeing through the illusions, and regained tighter control over my thoughts, feelings, and actions. And guess who partnered me throughout this journey of crests and troughs? The Buddha himself! Yes, arranged on my bookshelf is a graceful statue of the Buddha in silver that's embedded with sparkling stones. It is spesh because it was conferred on me by my alma mater as a token of appreciation for a professional training session that I conducted for them.

The Buddha classifies human beings into two broad categories – the worldlings, whose eyes are still covered with the dust of defilements and delusion; and the noble ones or the spiritual elite who obtain this status not from ecclesiastical authority but their inward nobility of character. While the promenade from bondage to deliverance, from worldliness to spiritual supremacy, is a graded path involving gradual practice and progress, it is not a uniform continuum, and this is best validated by natural selection. The idea of this book is to encourage us all to view ourselves and subsequently the world with a clearer lens and elevate to a level of equanimity where we can enjoy the cruise of life to the fullest.

To your fulfilment
Supriya Sharma

Contents

Chapter 1

Era of Secular Buddhism

'Religion is the impotence of the human mind to deal with occurrences it cannot understand.'

- Karl Marx

The harlequin world of 7 billion people that we exist in, is divided (united would have been the ideal word) into 18 major religious groups, Christianity topping the charts with 31.4% of the population being its adherents, followed by Islam at 23.2%, Hinduism at 15% and Buddhism at 7.1% (as per World Economic Forum data).

What's common among all these religions, whether chosen or inherited, is that they come in various denominations to act as kaleidoscopes through which we behold the beauties of creation. There's a peculiarity in diversity that the charming secularism dispenses. Just as there are varieties of Christianity, Islam, and Hinduism, there are different versions of Buddhism in Asia.

My rendezvous with Buddhism dates back to middle school, that too from a conventional angle, merely in the form of a supplementary reader which was a 50-page storybook about a prince from a wealthy family who lived during the 5th century BC and later gained popularity as 'the awakened one'. As a teenager, it was beyond my grey matter to comprehend what induced him to have decided to relinquish his lavish lifestyle and endure poverty and promote the idea of 'middle way' which means existing between two extremes, when the former didn't fulfil him. No wonder I inferred him to be a Homosapien from another planet who sought an unembellished life without social indulgences but also without deprivation, and eventually found enlightenment while meditating under a Bodhi tree, after six years of searching. Why under the Sun would someone desire to achieve that spiritual state and if one did, would it be scientifically justifiable or sustainable? This was no passing fancy but doubt that plagued my mind as I gained years. The inclination to grasp the strategic and tactical orchestration of a gigantic organization of seven continents called the 'world' has grown steeper as I experience the adulterated version of life.

With the globe shrinking into a village and simple being the new complex, the emergence of Western Buddhism in the United States and Europe has been an accepted trend. It consists of people who weren't born Buddhist but have chosen to adopt Buddhist tenets, meditation practice, in specific, sidelining the supernatural parts of Buddhism. Typical Asian Buddhist beliefs like you might be reincarnated as a hungry ghost in hell if things don't go well, or, if things go better you might wind up in heaven and spend years there before being reincarnated again might not make sense to the present-day humans with a scientific mindset based on solid reason as it is cumbersome to set up experiments that prove the validity of such hypotheses.

Interestingly, spiking curiosity among people about the true meaning of life in this fast-paced routine has led Buddhism to gain traction for addressing questions like - Why do people suffer? What is the underlying cause of sadness? Why do humans get anxious? Why do people behave contemptuously sometimes? Does the human mind deceive us about the nature of reality? And can the way the mind works be changed through meditation?

They form an authentic part of Buddhist heritage found in the earliest writings and are a common denominator of all Buddhisms. It is in the light of seeking answers to these questions that several people who are as like as chalk and cheese, regardless of their original religious affiliation have turned to what is commonly termed as 'Secular Buddhism'.

Chapter 2

A Naturalistic View

The mainstream purpose here isn't to deliberate on religions but to delve deeper into the abstractness associated with human life and how our actions are married to modern psychology. The naturalistic ideas in Buddhism pertain to the human mind, which makes them susceptible to scientific evaluation. These when titrated with psychology help people to gain clarity and assign meaning to their lives, give them moral orientation, offer consolation in times of sorrow, provide strength to tackle grief, and charge them with calmness as they encounter the turbulence of life.

William James, a great American psychologist broadly stated that the animating essence of religion is the belief that there exists an unseen order, and that our supreme good lies in harmoniously adjusting ourselves thereto. The unseen order referred to in Buddhism isn't precisely a cosmic plan, but the truth about the way things work, the truth about how reality is structured, the truth about human beings, even the truth about yourself.

The supposition that there is a truth behind things and a 'bottom' to the matter has drummed into all of us whether scientists, philosophers, theologians, or laypeople, a maniacal obsession about improving our explanatory capabilities defining the features of an intensively self-conscious, post-Cartesian world. While scepticism can be seen as the driving force behind science and technology as well as modern conceptions of faith and the soul, these truths often go unseen because the human mind contains certain built-in distortions. We have illusions that don't allow us to see the world transparently. Asserting that our supreme good lies in harmoniously adjusting ourselves to the normally hidden truth, Buddhism lays a path for this lyrical adjustment. It formulates what it considers to be the truth about reality. It tells us what we need to do to bring our lives in line with that reality and accept it wholeheartedly, in the bargain, relieving our suffering, in fact ending it altogether and, in the process, aligning ourselves with the moral truth.

Chapter 3

Connecting Buddhism & Evolution

For math buffs like me who are tempted to doubt the possibility of such alignment, let's refer to Kurt Gödel's incompleteness theorem, or - to use its full name – 'On Formally Undecidable Propositions of Principia Mathematica and Related Systems' published in 1931, which proves that within every mathematical system, you can invariably make statements that can neither be proved nor disproved within the system itself (hence "formally undecidable"). Put another way, no mathematical system, no matter how elegant or powerful, is complete. Don't you think this analogy fits well with the system of life as well?

The piece of mathematical jujitsu in consideration, proving unprovability formally (and elegantly) ended the strain of Western thought begun by Socrates and first fully-fledged out by Aristotle – the idea that intellectual inquiry will allow us to arrive at some fully knowable truth, that our picture of the universe can someday be complete.

The incompleteness theorem shows us that a complete understanding of the universe is impossible, even in theory. The ancillary effects of this revelation – a rejection of master narrative, an understanding that we will never have all the answers, an integration of contradiction, and an embrace of complexity – are freshly making themselves felt in the dawn of the 'post complete world, whether in religion or humankind.

The concept of evolution by selection encompasses natural selection, sexual selection, and selective processes that generate cultural evolution. It offers the best explanation for who we are, where we originated, and the nature of life in the rest of the universe. This modern psychology (evolutionary psychology) in some respects has been noted for lending support to the Buddhist ideas. For instance, it shows us that certain deceptions are built into the human mind and that we do suffer as a result, drawing from the study of how the human mind was programmed by natural selection. But to say that something is natural, or was engineered by natural selection, isn't to say that it's not permutable. If it were to be true, the theory of neuroplasticity won't have surfaced.

On the flip side of the same coin, the sheer audacity of Buddhism is alluring. It seems to run in opposition to some of the logic by which natural selection wired the brain, not to conclude that it's a complete rebellion against natural selection. It cleverly tends to do what might be termed as counterprogramming of the brain, in peculiarity, through such techniques as meditation that neutralize existing tendencies that were built into the brain by evolutionary selection.

The pertinent question is - Can the prescription laid out by Buddhism alleviate human suffering by making us see the world more clearly or whether dispelling the virally deep-seated illusions is the key to sustainable happiness?

Chapter 4

Emotions or Feelings?

If I would kick off a discussion on whether feelings and emotions are the same breeds, a majority would declare it to be bunkum. In other words, it is quotidian for people to use the terms 'feelings' and 'emotions' synonymously when they aren't interchangeable. While they are constituted of similar elements, there is a marked difference between the two of them, just as orange and Malta aren't the same fruit, though cousin-like.

A feeling is a conscious experience that comes through emotional or physical sensations like hunger or pain; although not every conscious experience, such as seeing or believing, is a feeling. An emotion manifests in the unconscious mind, it can only ever be felt through the sentimental experiences it gives birth to, even though it might be discovered through its accompanying symptoms - thoughts, beliefs, desires, and actions. It isn't uncommon for some beings to spend months and years, or even a lifetime, not understanding the depths of their emotions.

Well, are the feelings real? Why do our feelings have certain properties? Why did evolution create them that way? When does spiritual intelligence supersede emotional intelligence?

How do you define a feeling? It is something that you experience, right? So technically, as long as you're experiencing it, it is qualified to be real. Connecting these dots is a bewildering task, I've personally dodged it day in day out, now I acknowledge why – I placed my reality over the world's reality. Not far back in time, during European autumn, what Keats calls the season of mellow fruitfulness, I went through a period in life when I trusted my feelings more than ever. I began to perceive all my life events (and also the happenings in my mind) to be more real than they were, let them trespass into my core value system, and strategized my actions in accordance. I knew the path I was treading on wasn't the one I had chosen of the two roads that diverged in the dense woods, but I was habituated to it. I knew it wasn't going to take me anywhere, but I was determined to follow it. I knew life was too short to take the digressed route, but I was willing to allocate all my hours to it. That's the power of feelings, they can hypnotize you until you bang your head into a magic rock that opens up your eyes and takes you back to the drawing board. This indeed is an explicit part of the Buddhist thought that our feelings are not reliable guides to reality, they're not entirely trustworthy.

Won't it be life-changing to convince yourself that some of your most troublesome, unpleasant feelings aren't real and liberate yourself from them? When I say liberate, I mean freeing yourself from the shackles of feelings and living 'Sans Souci'. A huge assignment in itself, seemingly impossible at times but once you've hacked it, there is no one stopping you.

That's where meditation scores as a practical approach that critically distances you from your feelings or zips you through them, to avoid being misled by them. As you observe your mind, you can realize that your perception changes in a subtle way.

I was listening to an interview with a Buddhist Nun named Yifa, from Taiwan. She made it incredibly simple to assimilate that when we have great emotion, we tend to grasp that feeling as real because it is like a movie in continuity that we are watching on our internal televisions. But when we are contemplating on those sensations, we take them piece by piece and interestingly find that they are not real, not concrete. The fact remains that feelings can and do influence your perceptions (and actions in turn).

If you were shown a picture that looked like both a rope and a snake, what would you take it to be? There's a human tendency to make a snap judgement. Concerning this, an experiment has been conducted by researchers on how you can influence the judgements people make. Three sample populations were made to listen to happy music, no music, and scary music. Then they were shown the picture and asked what they saw there. While the happy music didn't have much of an effect one way or the other compared to just hearing no music, scary music had a pronounced effect. About 30% of the people who heard no music saw a snake as opposed to a coiled rope, and roughly 70% of the people who heard scary music thought they saw a snake.

Yes, nolens volens, the brain is assembled such so our feelings can browbeat our perceptions, just as in this contrived laboratory condition. It reminds me of a real-life story.

I was about to take a hike in Hong Kong in 2012 in what I learned was a banded krait terrain and I also had the information that a few years ago, a traveller who was bitten by a snake on a similar adventure died. The second piece of information changed my frame of mind altogether. As I took the walk along the trail, I was at least modestly fearful, and it reoriented the objects I was paying attention to.

The Greek playwright, Sophocles once said, "To a man who is afraid, everything rustles." And that's the point, you're going to be over-attentive to rustling sounds while hiking in that region based on the facts fed to you. And if you hear one and look down to see what's going on and suppose it turns out to be a lizard darting across your path, well it's a good chance, that for a second, you're going to think it's a snake. Or, if there happens to be an actual coiled rope as in that experiment, you will probably interpret that as a snake. From natural selection's point of view, such false positives make complete sense because it's better safe than sorry. Even if you prance out of the way 99 times out of 100 and it's not a snake, the same fear that made you do that imagining a snake that isn't there, makes sure that you jumped out of the way on the occasion when the snake is there. In that case, all that trouble of 99 times is worth it from natural selection's vantage point. This attests that the biology designs (which it doesn't obviously do in a conscious state) organisms ultimately for one purpose - to get their genes into the next generation, sounds mean but that's how we live. When would that happen? When we survive long enough. Natural selection hardly cares whether we see the world plainly or not, our brains aren't built to see the truth per se.

Drawing one basic parallel, Buddhism postulates that we should be sceptical of our feelings as they are not necessarily truthful guides to reality, and indeed, we should as well be sceptical of some of the thoughts and the perceptions those feelings foster. Likewise, evolutionary psychology also proposes a certain kind of scepticism, which is acceptable because we are not necessarily designed to encounter the truth. It's smack-dab tectonic to figure out exactly what the interactional dynamics are among our feelings, thoughts, and perceptions, and how they can collectively distort our view of the world.

Chapter 5

The Problem

The noble truths are foundational for the Buddhist thought to blossom. Akin to the elephant's foot-print, which on account of its hugeness, is supposed to seat the footprints of all other animals, the four noble truths, because of their comprehensiveness, are presumed to carry within themselves all the wholesome and beneficial teachings of the Buddha.

Building on an understanding of our feelings and what the convoying reality entails, the first and the second noble truths together constitute the Buddha's diagnosis of the human predicament. According to scriptures, the Buddha delivered them in a famous sermon at Deer Park shortly after attaining enlightenment, which is said to have happened after he meditated under a Bodhi tree for an exceedingly long time.

The first noble truth is usually translated into English as the "truth of suffering", which some people paraphrase as 'life is suffering', yes, perplexing it was when I heard so initially. Well, the Buddha didn't directly say 'life is dukkha', but that line does capture the essence that suffering is a permeating part of life, which I concluded after reading a good deal. Many scholars think that suffering doesn't adequately translate the fundamentalism in the word that the Buddha used. It isn't that the word is incorrect, it's just that it doesn't seize the full breadth of what may have incipiently been meant by the word, Duhkha (or Dukkha), which is typically translated as suffering. The two different spellings are language-specific, one for the Sanskrit version and the other for Pali (an ancient language closely related to Sanskrit).

The most nominated appurtenant translation of dukkha (or dukkha) is unsatisfactoriness in life. This meaning adds a layer of plausibility to the first noble truth as it buttresses the pervasiveness of suffering. As soon as this reaches your ears, you'll be tempted to shed an argument that it's not always that you suffer. Surely, whooping it up at your dream vacation - the Spanish islands of Ibiza with a serene background of turquoise waters, white sands, and splashing margaritas - is not suffering in any known way. However, if you add this sense of unsatisfactoriness to the word 'suffering', it's intelligible in a broad manner.

Let me make it more comprehensible. Any guess as to which is my favourite dessert? Belgian chocolate mousse it is, not minding extra ganache, buttercream, nut paste, or Jean Neuhaus' pralines. Though I restrict myself to only one chocolate mousse per week, I do go overboard while holidaying, consuming 3-4 servings in a go. This, of course, is followed by self-restraint to compensate for overdose. If you asked me, does eating that cocoa delight feels like suffering? Obviously not! You couldn't be kidding me. I'm not suffering. I am relishing it. Contrarily, it probably is true that just about as soon as I start swallowing the first bite, I'm already thinking about the next, kind of yearning for the bowl not to finish. And the fact that I want another mouse ministers that in an unvarnished coat, I didn't gain contentment. Theoretically, if you get satisfaction, you don't want any more. Euphoric, right?

There's always a moderate undercurrent of yearning no matter what we get. It feels pitch-perfect, to begin with, but eventually, the time comes when the thrill wears off, you want some more. A complimentary upgrade to business class from economy by your airline seems decorous at first, but not the second or third time; the expectations rise, you now want to be upgraded to first class. The pleasure doesn't last, and this business of things not lasting is a major theme of the Buddhist texts and is referred to as 'impermanence'. There's nothing in the world, which is permanent, certainly not pleasure, and yet we seem to cling to things. Strange, eh? Weren't humans supposed to be the most advanced version of animals, why such controversy then?

The second noble truth announces the cause of dukkha (or duhkha) - the cause of suffering and unsatisfactoriness in life. That cause precisely is, craving, it's a word that is comparable to thirst. Ever had that feeling of staggeringly missing your loved one who's 8,000 kilometres away on the map and you sense you'd die if they didn't appear in front of you at that very moment? It chokes you even more than if you were deprived of oxygen. How does not being able to breathe feel? Suffering in its true manifestation, isn't it?

And according to the Buddha, by clinging to things that won't last, we're evincing a kind of delusion. We're not getting the right picture about the impermanence of things. We're not reckoning with the truth about reality. The stakes of this go way beyond raw, sensory pleasures or gratifying things in general - reporting an A+ in the mid-semester exam, getting a glittery photoshoot, winning the esteem of your friends, or gaining the acclaim of society at large.

Whatever makes you feel grand, eventually that feeling will fade, and you're going to want more, by design. This wanting more and more of achievement used to be a consistent concern that I'd share with the personal coach throughout my MBA program. She would empirically attribute it to my specific personality type – a perfectionist achiever. The discussion never got to it being the way life is or the sweet-and-sour truth of life. Little did I know, this is what the psychologists refer to as the Hedonic Treadmill. 'Hedonic', meaning pleasure-seeking, and 'Treadmill', meaning you're at the same spot, not getting anywhere - you keep running and striving for happiness, but you don't step any closer to it.

The first two noble truths are not only about what we seek or desire, but they also cover anxieties and fears - anxieties about being criticized in public, going to a client meeting you don't want to go to, the fear of being eaten by a lion, the fear of being rejected by a potential mate or the fear of losing your life while skydiving. You typically won't want to include these under the rubric of craving, because you don't crave social rejection (unless you are an alien). You want to get away from that and not get closer to it. If you fear social criticism and you have anxiety about it, or if you have an uneasiness about performing badly at some presentation you're about to deliver, that's because it's your social status that you're clinging to. You're attached to your social status. If you fear a charging bull, that's because you are attached to your own existence, you cling to your own existence. Attachment is the key problem.

Getting off the boat? Buddhism is preaching one shouldn't be attached to one's own existence and the Buddha's diagnosis does explicitly include an attachment to your existence as part of the problem. It doesn't recommend that we cross the street without looking both ways though or come in front of a car raging at 125 km/hr on the expressway. It doesn't say that we should never be attracted to anything, or that we can never enjoy any pleasures. What it warns us against is clinging to things. It's like owning a licensed pistol but not using it, come what may.

Chapter 6

The Delusive Pleasure

As the second noble truth proposes, the source of suffering and unsatisfactoriness is our craving - our pursuit to hang onto branches that would eventually wither and won't last, including pleasure. Our failure to grasp this dynamic is simply another example of our failure to see the world clearly. Pleasure does evaporate (multiple times a day), and it is human to have much trouble accepting that. The brain is constructed in such a way that pleasure is fleeting, but a close examination of our actions would reveal that we focus a lot more on pleasure than fleetingness.

In Buddhist writing, when the Buddha calls attention to our failure to see things transparently, he often wields a literally glossed word, 'delusion'. This may be like tooting an overstatement, for example, when I'm gazing at chocolate mousse (that you now know I consume once every week), there's no fraction of a second when I'm visualizing it to be a foreign agent conspiring to assassinate me or something sphinxlike. Am I thinking that it will last forever? Do I think it will last for only ten minutes? Probably no. As I look forward to relishing the mousse, I'm celebrating a lot more about the pleasure than about the evaporation of that pleasure. And I'm certainly not getting to the sugar rush subsiding, leaving me unsettled. I'm focused on that targeted moment of pleasure, the D-moment.

Well, something more comparable to delusion may actually happen with infatuation. If you've ever had a sincere crush on someone, you'd recall that you had a pretty distorted view of the world, it looked all pink. You had serious trouble spotting any blemishes or deficiencies in the person. All you wanted was to be with that person or speak to them. It was all beautiful, right? And there was this believed abstraction that, wow, should you ever be so lucky to find yourself in a relationship with that person, everything would be rosy, probably eternally. It was an undiluted delusion. Relationships, needless to say, are, sibylline, holding together the arcane network of humans.

If you genuinely want a particular job with your dream multi-national company, you look forward to it, you muse on all the great perks it's going to bring and how your career would be boosted for good. In that hallucination, you lose sight of the hassles underlying that job, and you begin to believe that if you can just pass that job interview, then you can relax as you will have arrived. For sure, you won't have indubitably bobbed up. The gratification is not going to last for as long as you presume. It never lasts forever.

Have a look at the parts of the brain that are party to the failure of gratification lasting forever. One barefaced candidate would be our faddish neurotransmitter, dopamine. You assumably have read about dopamine as the pleasure chemical of the reward chemical. The true endocrinological story is that the effects of dopamine depend on the part of the brain embroiled, which neurons are involved, which receptors are involved, and so on. There's also the discrepancy - does dopamine actually cause pleasure, or is it just correlated with pleasure?

But what's the motive of pleasure being so fleeting? Why have our brains been schematized in that fashion? Why isn't that dopamine spigot left on? You could keep dishing out dopamine for a long period of time, but that doesn't happen. Why is that so? And why do we seem not to sponge up the picture in our everyday lives about how expeditiously the pleasure is going to drain off? The sole answer lies with evolutionary psychology, which has a singular goal and continually works towards it - getting the genes into the next generation.

The three associated principles of such design by natural selection can be decoded here. With animals (as with humans), elevating the social status, food and sex are the basic requirements. When these goals are met, the animal should get some pleasure. Pleasure is what reinforces the behaviour, makes them more likely to do whatever led them to the goal in the first place. This is the first principle. Then, number two, the pleasure should not last forever. Obviously, if you ate one indulging meal and just blissed out to never feel the unpleasant sensation of hunger again, you won't ever eat again, and you would die.

Or, if you procreated and then just basked in the afterglow for a long time, thinking about how seductively groovy it had been, and meanwhile, in your species, some other organism cracked it, found it was great, but began to feel restless, and went on to get some more food or do something to elevate the social status - that animal is going to transfer more genes into the next generation than you will. These restlessness genes, for not being satisfied for long, that the particular animal has are going to do better than your genes (survival of the competitive). The third principle of design is that the animals should focus more on the pleasure that reaching the goals will bring, than on the subsequent evaporation of pleasure.

Obviously, if your eyes are twinkling for that prominent star by the name of 'pleasure', if you're homing in on how good it's going to feel to reach the goal, you'll reach the destination. Whereas if you're sitting there reasoning, pleasure's going to be over in a microsecond, why work so hard? In that case, you're going to seemingly wind up sitting in your room alone, full of ennui. And that's definitely not going to get your genes into the next generation. Taking calculated risk is what investment professionals might compare it to. These principles of design make sense in terms of natural selection, and they resonate with the Buddhist teaching too.

The Buddha claimed that pleasure tends to evaporate, and it leaves us unsatisfied, and it perfectly conveys the impression that pleasure is blueprinted to vanish so it will leave us unsatisfied and letching for more. This unsatisfaction will motivate us to go out and do more work and check off more bullet points on natural selection's agenda. Plus, Buddhism states that humans tend to focus on pleasure and not on the fleetingness of pleasure, which over and above ties well into the theory of natural selection.

I'd like to exercise my free will here, which philosophers have struggled to reconcile with the terrestrial, deterministic views of nature advanced by science. Epicurus insisted that there must be some element of randomness within nature that allows the free will to exist, what he better called 'the swerve'. To put it directly, there have been times in my journey where this Buddhism-supported psychological facet of humans focusing on pleasure and not on evaporation of pleasure was contradicted, when my genuine concern was lasting of pleasure as opposed to the pleasure itself, which seemed reasonable as my rational mind found it immensely helpful to weigh the gain in both scenarios while decision making, and I can claim that the initial grief inflicted by depriving oneself of that pleasure saves from copious amounts of future pain in those cases.

By the way, anticipation doesn't come under the umbrella of pleasure, it is outside of it as it pertains to imagining the actual pleasure that you're going to experience when you get the reward. I return to one of my vices, high-calorie beverages. Every afternoon, I have a rich two and ten-ounce latte, which is 210 calories. I could easily manage with a similar cup of cappuccino, which would be 130 calories. While haggling with projects and negotiating with clients, the time comes when I call a shot that

I deserve it for all the revenue I've been attracting since morning. And I'm musing about it, I can taste it, I can visualize the cream slurping through my lips, it's as fulfilling as a passionate clinch. I climb upstairs to the coffee machine, I get it. I may, in a habitude, not experience any pleasure at all beyond this point. The whole operation has become so automatic that I may just be pondering over frivolous matters, chatting with my colleagues about random stuff, or if alone, my mind may be wandering, or I may be on a call with a supplier as I sip it up. But what happens if I skip it someday? Can I get the same satisfaction only by thinking of a latte and not letting it down my oesophagus?

If I would conjecturally relate this to another experience, it'd be like I'm in a shopping mall, I see a spunky black dress by Versace, I'm thinking about buying it. It's all fantastically gorgeous! I go and grab it, head to the trial room to see how the fitting is. Che bella! It's as if it was made to accentuate my curves. I take it to the counter, I buy it. And then I come home and wear it again and, yeah, it's okay. But each successive trial is less okay, I am getting used to the new dress, it's becoming normal. At this point, I've done the work (as per the definition of work in Physics too). The motivational gear has gotten me to take the necessary action to acquire the dress, to reach the goal. It's fine, however, the anticipation was probably where most of the pleasure happened when I thought of clubbing in Buenos Aires donning that dress. This is quite speculative motivational dynamics that we would expect from a brain built on the technical measurements.

Now, the question arises, why would natural selection have sketched brains that are attracted to chocolate mousse - it's not too good for us, right? And the hint is, natural selection didn't, because after all, chocolate mousse was not appearing in the landscape when our lineage evolved. What was part of the scenery was just sweetness. Natural fruits had sweetness, fruits were beneficial for us, and so that seems to be why we have a sweet tooth that can now go overboard and touch profanity.

To analyze this process in the stone age perspective when there were no fancy desserts, imagine one of our distant ancestors spotting some trees at a distance, which look like fruit trees. It's a scorcher, it's a long walk, they don't feel like putting in the effort. But the structures they are seeing could be fruit trees, they remember the taste of this fruit, get a teensy-weensy spike of dopamine that motivates them to go and investigate. They take a trek and reach there. There is plenty of fruit, they eat it, get a few more drops of pleasure. They may not need oodles of pleasure, but enough for a little reinforcement, and here, you know the biological brain has done its job. In cases where we are sufficiently used to the pleasure we're getting, it becomes routinized, let's say closing a million-dollar sale every month, so that often there's little, if any, pleasure in the actual achievement and more pleasure in the anticipation.

Then why not just do the anticipation and skip the actual achievement? Smart work therapy, eh? Don't they say work smart, not hard? That's where the joy is anyway, agree? The reason it won't deliver results is the letdown of unfulfilled anticipation. You've probably done this before, gone to the refrigerator on the next day of your birthday, searching for that piece of blueberry-pineapple cake that was specially baked for the occasion. You open it to find somebody has eaten the cake. Blah! You not only feel an absence of pleasure, but you're also let down, which does serve as a motivational device situationally.

Why pleasure doesn't last and leaves us unsatisfied, longing for more is boldly explained by evolution. It also clarifies enigmatically why pleasure is our nucleus and not the fleetingness of pleasure, as Buddhism suggests as well. In all cruelty, natural selection doesn't gauge our happiness meter the way we do. It utilizes happiness as a tool to guide us. If making us gay at one moment will keep us motivated, good. If making us forsaken, if making us unsatisfied, if making us suffer, will get us to do the work that's on its agenda, that's better. This is one of the key aspects in which Buddhism casts a shadow of rebellion on natural selection.

My take on it - happiness is the vitality of my being, it is within me, and as a consequence, I am not comfortable with the idea of suffering or being unhappy, but I ponder at times - would we appreciate happiness as much as we do if there wasn't a tinge of unhappiness in life? It's much easier said than done though. I realize that Buddhism wants us to behold the world patently in all we do and aspires to end our suffering (which is partially achievable in my own experience) while evolutionary science wants us to sometimes not see the world clearly and suffer. Which way you want to go is a matter of decision-based on reasoning and conditioning. Whatever decision-making tool you use, be it Force Field Analysis, Decision Tree, SWOT (Strengths, Opportunities, Weaknesses & Threats), Kepner Tregoe, etc., remember that decisions are simply choices, but these choices are strong enough to define your life.

Chapter 7

The Solution

While the first and the second noble truths are focused on the problem, the third and the fourth noble truths are solution-bound and contain the Buddhist prescription, the cure for what ails mankind.

The bad news from the first noble truth is that human life is full of suffering and unsatisfactoriness, and the positive news from the second noble truth is that there is at least a cause that has been isolated, the basal cause of suffering, i.e., craving, clinging to entities or notions that are not going to last forever.

Then comes into the scene the doctor to treat us as per diagnosis in phases one and two. The third noble truth unveils the cure for suffering, i.e., the abandonment of craving and of clinging. The fourth noble truth becomes handy while flowcharting the path you must follow if you're going to attain full liberation, which is called the Eightfold Path or the Astangika-marga cemented on ethical behaviour and virtue cultivation. According to this, there are eight points to be mastered if you want to be liberated, which aren't necessarily about an oppressive list of dos and don'ts or the hang-up about moral conduct that the Abrahamic or Hindu religions are considered to have. They are - right view, which pertains to getting a proper understanding of the Buddhist teaching as a cicerone to the nature of things; right intention; right speech in the form of avoiding verbal misdeeds such as gossiping, divisive and senseless speech; right action to refrain from physical misdeeds such as killing, stealing, and sexual misconduct; right livelihood by avoiding trades that directly or indirectly harm others; right effort as in abandoning negative states of mind and harbouring positive states, right mindfulness; and right concentration.

Crawling to the meditative part of the path is an uphill battle, requires heavy lifting to be done, serious backbreaking work to put it straight, as to get to liberation, we're supposed to abandon craving and clinging, we're supposed to lose our aversion to unpleasant things, which obviously is no cakewalk. For me, meditation isn't the only ingredient that goes into cultivating that genre of discipline, but is a major fraction of the pie, as spiced up by the advancement it has gained among informed global citizens in recent years. Did you ever notice retreats being shown much love, giving a head bump to adrenaline-rush activities like skiing or diving? Well, I didn't. If you want to touch Nirvana (enlightenment) and view the essence of lucent reality as the Buddha taught it, a sagacious trick to doing that is to back up in the first factor of the path, i.e., the right view, that's when you gain an intellectual percipience of the Buddhist credo. But it's in the meditative zone where you gain an experiential understanding of the Buddhist doctrine. So, it's as good as learning how to drive a car at a driving school classroom first before actually taking the steering to the road. But mind the catch here, our Nirvana mechanism slides backwards. For example, let's recall the oft-heard idea of impermanence. When you meditate, it leads you to gain an intuitive apprehension of the impermanence of things - the impermanence of your feelings, your thoughts, rather everything that comes into your mind, and this apprehension, in turn, reinforces the intellectual understanding of the Buddhist doctrine and strengthens your commitment to it.

I am not a meditation expert, rather inferior to an amateur if it was to be put hierarchically, but this is what I think of it. Meditative practice is being on a kind of spectrum, on one end of which is the strictly therapeutic practice of low wavelength. Some people in my circle return from work knackered, do ten to fifteen minutes of meditation at home and feel lighter, that's it. They don't swot any of the Buddhist doctrines clubbed with meditation. And then on the other end of the spectrum, there's Nirvana, the high wavelength game, way down there, where you enter a domain that can be fairly called spiritual practice, the motivation behind which is not only self-help but there is a pining to become a supernal individual, to support others, and to vivify the transparency of the world.

Additionally, as a result, one is imparted with a realization that there's an organic kinship between becoming a better person and seeing the world more sharply, between self-help and helping others so to say, thus completing a positive feedback loop as it kindles a predilection to strip yourself off some of the delusions and misperceptions that seem to be natural for human beings in the process of becoming a better person. Here, your aim is to organize the multiple alignment fibre between the truth about the world, the truth about other people, about yourself, and the moral truth. What comes as a bonus is you reduce your suffering in the chain. You'll figure out there is a privy progression from taking care of yourself to becoming a more considerate version of yourself.

Remember the Sci-Fi movie, The Matrix, depicting a dystopian future with enough visual bravado and heavy special effects brooding paranoia? When the character played by Keanu Reeves realizes that he and everyone on the planet are admittedly living in a dream world and their perceived reality is just a hallucination inflicted on them by their robot overlords, he joins a rebellion to attain complete liberation. My American friends allegorically call it a dharma movie.

Think about it, what would your consciousness be like if you disrobed it of all the misperceptions and delusions that seem to be built into us by natural selection? If you've ever meditated, what was your first impression like? That you weren't made for it? That it suits the ascetic life high up in the undisturbed tranquil mountains away from the materialistic world? You must have had doubts about how this act of sitting in one place with closed eyes could lead to mental peace. How could it bring clarity to your vision?

How could it pacify your mangled soul? The answer lies in mastering the meditative technique once you've gotten it by nuts and bolts, followed by practice, practice, practice, and more practice; teleporting you to a world that looks and feels way different than the one you live in – as clear as a crystal. Meditation isn't about stopping the thoughts from flowing within us, but simply acknowledging each thought and letting it flow fluidly. But when you get to that higher plane, don't get attached to the pleasure. Now you know why!

When I commenced meditation, not willingly, to be frank, but because the business school I was studying at was deliberate in promoting mindfulness as a critical component of leadership development; I would always complain of my mind not being calm, not being in a zero state with all sorts of thoughts dancing a contemporary mix of salsa and capoeira. I had misconstrued the practice of meditation, resultantly I meditated several times questioning the worth of this practice and feeling it wasn't sufficiently rewarding to sustain it. Eventually, as I deciphered the gravitational pull of the technique, I was able to differentiate the leading indicators from the lagging ones. Building on this, I pressed my customization button choosing what resonated with my core and went on with non-traditional dynamic methods of meditation like golfing (whose methodology is way cavernous than it looks on the surface).

Your mileage counts on who you are as a person, your personality, your upbringing, you're toning up, and your environment. When meditation gains momentum, it energizes you with a skill set that grants you the fortitude to go through physical and emotional discomfort with greater poignancy, but less problem, you basically learn how to escape into discomfort, rather, embrace it with open arms.

Pallidly, there are two ways to deal with discomfort. Escape from it if you can. And if you can't, it's good to have in your quiver of life arrows the ability to escape into it. Then you can have the cake and eat it too. You experience the richness of being human, a part of which is uncomfortable and whose magnitude is a function of your sensitivity. It has served as a coolant in my radiator on several occasions. When you're feeling sad or on the border of being depressed, sit down, close your eyes, and make an attempt to accept it. Even if you don't wish to have your eyes shut, seclude yourself in a solitary corner, or engage in a relaxing activity. And just say, bring it on. Do not fight with the discomfort, you're not in the wrestling ring. What is making you sad? What does sadness feel like? Pay attention to it, accept it. Examine that feeling of sadness and get closer to it, embrace it with grace. Let it get diluted in your purest self. You'd sense diminishing of the suffering; you'd have made peace with it; it won't stress you anymore if you know what I mean.

My personal hack for doing this is Ikebana, the Japanese art of flower arrangement dating back to the Heian period when floral offerings were made at altars. When I face encumbrance due to a vicious issue that seems unresolvable through gentle self-talk or a problem that seems mightier than a monster, I engrossed arrange twigs, blooms, and other foliar elements, piece by piece, carefully following the specified angles, making exquisite alterations, accepting the fact that the situation is not within my circle of control and the solution doesn't lie in my hands, but doing the job beautifully as if the storm is settling down, releasing my fear, letting the bitter-sweet acceptance of pain and suffering percolate down my nerves. It has a surprising healing effect. Like everything else, it didn't furnish desired outcomes in my debut run, there were multiple iterations required.

Therefore, meditation doesn't necessarily have to be at home or in a quiet setting, do it your own way. For example, you can find yourself in a supermarket getting frustrated because the elderly lady in front of you is taking so long, she forgot her credit card in the car and got to know this only on getting to the cash register. Once you decide to look at this feeling of irritation and observe it, it loses its power over you and dissolves, like an alum rock humbly dissolves in water.

Categorically, each Buddhist tradition has a meditation type associated with it, for instance, Tibetan Buddhists, when they meditate, they do a lot of visualizing of images. Zen Buddhists meditate on koans, the cryptic or paradoxical sayings or questions with their eyes open, sitting down, looking at a wall or candle. In the Vipassana style of meditation, which is particularly common in Southeast Asia, there's ample emphasis on observing the working of your mind. Attending a week-long Vipassana based retreat on a scenic island may be an equanimous experience for mind mastery enthusiasts. Did you know there are stereotypes about the people who practice the traditions? Out of curiosity, I stumbled on a blog that read that Tibetan meditation is for artists, Zen is for poets, and Vipassana is for psychologists. And if you are a hyper-creative individual, dare to combine the three.

Chapter 8

Is Nirvana a Reality?

Typically, there are two hallmarks of a mystical experience of enlightenment (or Nirvana as it is aesthetically termed). First, it is noetic, and second, it is ineffable. By noetic, the Buddha meant that there is a sense that knowledge has been imparted. Then the ineffable part corresponds to infinity, it isn't describable, similar to the stillness that penetrates universal awareness.

Has someone other than the Buddha himself actually attained liberation? That's the question which popped up in my mind as I landed on a work by Robert Wright, a religious scientist where I watched him interview a highly esteemed Theravada Buddhist monk ordained in Sri Lanka named Bhikkhu Bodhi, who has written the 2000 pages of translation and commentary of discourses of the Buddha. Here's an excerpt from the dialogue between the interviewer and the monk.

> Robert: Have you attained liberation?
> Bhikkhu Bodhi: No, not by a long shot.
> Robert: Are there people alive today who you think have attained liberation?

> Bhikkhu Bodhi: I would say that is quite possible, maybe some monks in Thailand, Burma, or a few in the forests of Sri Lanka.

It sounded as intriguing as the search for dinosaurs. I would surely want to witness how the liberated individuals look like. Does their skin resemble ours or are they made up of pulverized flesh and blood?

Assuming you're among the many of us who have not attained enlightenment and you're imagining it; I feel no-frills experiences would be good candidates to get a flavour of the basic elements of enlightenment.

Normally, there is an impression of separation between you and the people and objects in the world. With enlightenment, it gets diminished as continuity is introduced. You begin to think that to harm others would be to harm yourself. In other words, you start to doubt that there's any real difference between your interests and their interests. But you know from natural selection's point of view this is absolute hearsay. There's a contradiction somewhere that is built into the system by natural selection. If this planet is full of people whose perceptual machinery was designed based on the premise that each of them is more important than the rest, then, obviously contradictions will arise, because that is itself an internally contradictory premise. It can't be the case that they're all more important than everyone else.

It isn't fortunate that we tend to feel short-lived

sparks of enlightenment akin to orgasms when it should have been a state of being. Thankfully, there is such thing as partial liberation which has brought together several scientists and philosophers to take up the challenge to scrutinize the Buddhist ideas about the human mind. Research in this field has been picking up momentum. In support, a few months back, it was in the news that meditation increases gamma wave activity. You may have also read that over time, the amount of white matter in the brain can rise with meditation.

Indeed, knowledge increases through synergy – through the spreading activation of millions of neurons, and families of neurons distributed among thinking individuals. The virtual universities of mind dedicated to creating balanced lives, in bringing individuals with a common intellectual foundation into sufficient proximity to allow for rich communication, cause jumps across metaphorical collective neurons – signals that then propagate through the society of neurons (a' la Minsky) and create new knowledge. This can be summarized as - if you can't eliminate all your suffering, you can eliminate some of it. If you can't reach complete equanimity, you can get more tranquillity and balance than you have now, and your life can change considerably, or even be transformed.

In a paper published in the proceedings of the National Academy of Sciences, there is a detailed description of the brain activity when people meditate. It renders the default mode network quieter and less active. Imagine yourself marching down the street not doing anything in particular. Even then, there's actually a whole lot going on in your brain. You're thinking about yourselves usually. You might be regretting something you did in the past or worrying about something that's coming up, or planning for something, at times, even fantasizing - there is significant action happening in our brains. The automatic network gets activated, or co-activated when we're up to these types of self-referential processing tasks. In a spatial sense, it does take your mind somewhere other than where you are, which causes you to lose focus on your immediate environment when the network is active. Funny enough, it does so in a temporal sense along the dimension of time as well.

Coming back to meditation, what purpose does it serve then? As you meditate, the default mode network gets quiet, because after all, one way to phrase the main point of meditation is mindfulness - be here now. Does it remind you of the title of a famous book that was published in the 1970s about meditation and spirituality (if at all you were born at that time or by any chance if you read the book later)?

I find it jocular when I am focusing on my breath and suddenly a thought bubbles up - what about this email I've got to write later today to a client who has delayed the payment for my services? It's kind of delicate, how should it be handled, bearing in mind that I don't want to spoil the relationship we've built over time. Or, I'll think of a helper I may have offended a couple of days ago and wonder how I can make amends. Or credit card payment due date could be on the tracks. It is also possible to think about somebody you have a romantic inclination for, and how you can impress them when you meet them in a couple of days. It could be anything. As effortless as it may seem, thinking isn't an exercise to be taken for granted; it is a vertiginous luxury. 11 million bits are sent by the human body per second to the brain for processing, yet the processing capacity of the conscious mind is only 50 bits per second.

Didn't I mention I used to be worried that distraction in the course of meditation happens with me alone? Later as I got in touch with meditators around the world, I heaved a sigh of relief when they shared similar stories from their initial days. The science behind it points to the default mode network doing its job. It takes advantage of free time, if you're not engaged in a task that requires focus like playing a sport, writing a report, making calculations, or just looking at somebody and recollecting where did you meet them - if you're not doing one of such things that require conscious focus, then, that's free time, in a way. And the nimble default mode network uses that time, usefully may be in a satirical intendment, to take care of your grand enterprise - your private business, your social business, and your professional business.

When this network gets silenced during meditation, it doesn't necessarily imply you've entered a state of mindfulness. It certainly is a basic first step towards mindfulness for the network to calm down, for you to get beyond the self-involvement that the network keeps you enmeshed in; but to orbit in a state of mindfulness, there's a second dimension in which you have to escape self-involvement, to look at something mindfully, look at it objectively, not from your ordinary subjective telescope.

If regression analysis of mindfulness were to be conducted, here's how it would be done. Think of a colleague you don't like and see if you can just look at the feeling of dislike and not get petrified, not let it divert your train of thought to avoid winding up rehearsing a litany of grievances against the person or plotting revenge against the person. In that case, you're closer to a state of mindfulness. If you're able to sort this out, won't it make your professional life (personal also) a soft-pedal, and allow your productivity to tick up the dial? The brain circuits are diagrammed to get us to focus on things that matter to us, whether positive or negative. The more they matter in quantity, the stronger is the feeling in quality. What you pay attention to, expands. Therefore, it is worthy for your awareness to be occupied by such meaningful things that elicit a strong reaction, and it is none other than the default mode network that tends to inject them into your consciousness.

So next time when you're walking down the street, do this - consciously be on guard for things that you don't normally pay attention to. Those things will depend on what demographic you're in. Suppose you're a young heterosexual female with an eye for well-built young males and especially if you find them attractive, paying even more attention to them, and you probably pay little attention to young females, size them up, compare them to yourself, they are after all in some way the competition; start paying attention to elderly people next time. One thing you'll find is that it's bothersome and unnatural to focus on these people because you don't care much about them. But you may also find that if you do pay attention to them, it's easier to appraise them calmly. Our unconscious mind often excludes from our awareness the things that we're not that interested in. We see what we want to see. This explains why it is unnatural to just walk down the street with a truly mindful attitude toward everything we're paying attention to.

Training your perception on the affective reaction (which mindfulness induces) is profoundly anti-Darwinian. Fundamentalists who still don't believe in evolution would support this slant which seems like the strongest way to give a middle finger to our selfish genes, and in the bargain, depriving the reaction of its power.

Chapter 9

Can Feelings be Trusted?

How about giving mindfulness (or presence in the moment) an opportunity to address these questions from the initial chapters - Are the feelings real? Can they be trusted?

Viewing the world mindfully can change your relationship to your feelings, simple chemistry. But does this changed relationship to your feelings actually help you see the world with more clarity? To answer this, it would pay to know the parameters at inception, meaning what the relationship between these feelings and reality was primordial. Were the feelings by the slightest measure reliable guides to reality?

According to the Buddha, there are tones or shades associated with feelings - there are pleasant feelings, unpleasant feelings, and neutral feelings. The evolutionary function of feelings and the reason appended to the existence of feeling tones was later explored by a biologist named George Romanes who wrote 'The Origin of Species'. He stated that pleasure and pain must have been evolved as the subjective accompaniment of processes that are respectively beneficial or injurious to the organism, that the organism should seek the one and shun the other.

It implies that basic feelings are molecularly based on the concepts of approach and avoidance, or at least were about that in the first instance when they arose. Dollars to doughnuts, it is consistent with human experience, isn't it? If there's something you want to ward off, like a scorpion, it gives you a bad feeling, a feeling of aversion, or if there's something you approach, like a colourful spring painting, it gives you a shipshape feeling, a feeling of fascination.

Surprisingly enough, in the Buddha's teaching, no word translates to emotions as a generic category, though emotions and feelings come in the same bouquet. With humans, feelings directly motivate behaviour. If your finger winds up in an open flame, you're going to feel the burn and retract it rapidly with the teamwork of sensory and motor neurons. However, sometimes feelings influence human behaviour more indirectly. Thinking of someone you hate; you start thinking about all the things that they've done wrong. That may have no hair-trigger impact on your behaviour, but down the road, when you're talking to a third person about them, you've got your arsenal ready. You can say all these nasty statements about them and undermine their status.

Like it or not, we are designed to be slaves of our feelings. They reach out and hold us by the neck. They paralyze our logic. They pull our thought strings, they regulate our behaviour, we feel their impact. When we meditate, they become less substantial, reduce in weight, and lose their grip. They begin to feel ethereal; they have no impact.

In Darwinian relativity, if the purpose of feelings is to steer us away from things that are bad for us and to steer towards things that are good for us, then you might put into words that feelings are judgments about things in the environment as to whether harmful or profitable for us plus the associated behaviour. Feelings are the encoding of our judgments about the environment, and judgments can be true or false. Can we state with certainty that natural selection is efficient at doing its job? Do our feelings pretty reliably manoeuvre us towards things that are good for us and drive us away from things that are grungy? And your knee-jerk response followed by pause and reflection would be – it depends.

Sometimes, we land up in an environment that natural selection didn't prepare us for. We're living in a radically transformed surrounding that's nothing like the one we were carved for, and that can influence whether feelings are labelled as true or false. I earlier alluded to one example of this, chocolate mousse. I am aware that mousse isn't really great for me, but why am I attracted to it? Well, because in the environment in which humans evolved, sweet edibles like fruits were generally healthy. There wasn't any junk food. So, this sweet tooth that made absolute sense in that environment, can, in this environment, lead us to act against our best interest.

Another relevant example is rage. If you ask an evolutionary psychologist the story behind rage and what is the rage for, they'll probably give such a narration - in the period of our evolution, in a hunter-gatherer village, it was very important for you to send the message that you were not to be exploited or taken advantage of and that if people tried to steal your mate or steal your food or disrespect you, there would be a price to be paid. It was totally worth getting in a fight with people over these essentials. This was the message for everyone you're going to be dealing with on a regular basis, from here on watching what happens when someone tries to mess up with you, so it's all the more worthwhile from the point of view of your long-term interests to fight somebody over your honour, or over respect; even if that incurs some damage to you, as long as they pay a price too.

If we analyze the absurd case of road rage according to our present lifestyle, in Darwinian scope, we might end up in a conclusion 180 degrees apart. You're sitting in your car and the other vehicle bumps into you. You get infuriated and throw shouts at the driver who dented your motor. The person whom the rage is directed toward is someone you're never going to see again, so there's hardly any value in sending a message to them. Everyone who's watching this, the other drivers, or commuters, you're never going to see them again as well so there isn't any point whatsoever in pursuing this rage. You might argue that this person had committed some transgression, so your rage was warranted, but then you're veering into questions of moral truth. This shows how a changing ecosystem influences a feeling that at one point could be described as trustworthy, and it suddenly ceases to be meaningful.

If our feelings can't be trusted as accurate, then it is outright logical to evaluate them mindfully, i.e., objectively, and decide which ones you're going to let get traction, which ones you're going to engage with. Viewing feelings with discernment is what we refer to as wisdom.

Chapter 10

Does the Self Exist?

The idea that the 'self', the candidate we are aware of being inside of us and demanding utmost attention does not exist, is hard to fathom. I wonder what the fate of a fella would be who tells you in your face that you don't exist, while you stand intact in bones and skin.

Jung Chaw, a famous Buddhist monk from Thailand once warned against intellectualizing this idea. He wrote that if you used your wit to judge this canon by having somebody lecture about it or read about it, your head will explode. Now that beggar's belief!

Buddha laid out the concept of 'not-self in a star sermon: 'The Discourse on the Not-Self', which is said to be the second sermon he delivered after his enlightenment. The first one was 'The Discourse on the Four Noble Truths'.

What explicitly did the Buddha mean by the self, which doesn't even exist? Who are we then? If you delve into the prevailing Indian philosophical discourse of the time and gather what the word would have meant to the Buddha, it might leave you decently persuaded. The other is proof by contradiction, exactly following suit with mathematical theorems. Consider this analogy, if you were an archaeologist from a future civilization and you came across the term 'Santa Claus', not knowing what it meant; and then you came across a lecture evangelizing that Santa Claus doesn't exist because no man can visit a million homes or more in a single night. What would you conclude? By the way, I still find Santa's gift underneath my pillow on waking up on Christmas morning, not sure who at my home does it for me, but it definitely cheers me up and puts a contagiously big smile on my face. On a serious note, if you were this archaeologist, you could infer that the Santa Claus character must have been someone who was primarily thought to visit a million or more homes in a night, right? That would be a valid inference.

A comparable assessment can be done for the Buddha's argument about not-self. The best way to experience the not-self is through meditation, fitly feeling the truth of the doctrine, and becoming convinced that there is no substance called 'self' inside you. In theory, there are five aggregates or heaps of clinging, the five material and mental factors that give rise to craving and clinging, according to the Buddhist thought. They fudge together everything there is about a person, including the person's body, the person's mind, and the person's experience – form (applies to anything physical in the world, in this context, it is the person's physical body), feeling (sensation), perception, mental formations (volitional activities) and consciousness (the phenomenon of subjective awareness).

Referring to the standard interpretation of this discourse on the not-self, the Buddha talks about the properties that the aggregates seem to have, and these properties are not compatible with the properties we associate with the self. Hence, the self could not be.

Could you show where the self is? If I consider myself, I think of a self that was intact when I was sweet sixteen, and it's the same self I have now. Though I've changed a lot since I was sixteen in form and mental formations precisely, but fundamentally, there has been some essence in me that intuitively accounts for continuity of identity. We do consider the self, in a commonsensical way, as being something solid or essence that endures through time. With much flux, everything is changing all the time in all the five aggregates, so, it's hard to imagine a substantially persistent self-being there.

The Buddha actually twines self with control. Principally, when he elaborates on control, he doesn't mean what we guess he might, about the self and control - the CEO Rule - the one that asserts control. In this sermon, he mentions that self's house should be in order, which implies that there is also a controller within the self. Supporting this, there's a story about a character named Augavesinna, who denies the Buddha's teaching on the self. He claims, "Feeling is self, perception is self, mental formations are self." He confronts the Buddha, confident that he can win the debate. He repeats, "Yes this is self." The Buddha handles him tactfully saying, "Okay, tell me Augavesinna, is it in the power of the king to say within his domain who should be executed or who should be banished?" Augavesinna replies, "Of course it is, and he should have that power", to which the Buddha continues, "Well tell me, do you have the power to say of the form of your body? Let my body be like this, or let my body be like that." Augavesinna falls in silence. He doesn't utter a word. The Buddha asks him again. Augavesinna still doesn't speak, and then, the Buddha brings out a rule that I didn't know existed. He reveals, "You have to comprehend there is this rule that if someone refuses to answer a well-founded question asked by the Buddha three times in a row, that person's head will be split into seven pieces." And as if to drive this home, a spirit appears above Augavesinna's head, plying an iron thunderbolt, and intimidates to split his head open. This is how proximate anyone has ever come to actually having their head explode, as Jung Chaw warned while trying to apprehend the hard-to-digest concept of not-self. Finally, Augavesinna gives in agreeing with the Buddha, "You're right, I ultimately do not have control over my body."

The self is about persistence through time, like a solid core that persists, which lacks throughout the aggregates, and is therefore contradictory to the concept of being in charge, as discussed under the umbrella of leadership (knowledge of self).

Paradoxes pertaining to metaphysical doctrines arise in various religions and philosophical systems, causing the thinkers to come along and purport to resolve them. Within the Buddha's liberative framework or the framework of contemplative insight, he teaches that one should excogitate all the constituents of being as not mine, not I, not myself. But in another context of ethical action or the context of karma and its fruit (as proposed by the Bhagavat Gita), the Buddhist teaching remains a style of framing the issue productively, as instrumental and pragmatic.

In practice, if you happen to slap your friend in an event of contradiction or fight, you need to own it up, you cannot say it wasn't you who committed the action (going by the not mine theory). Ironically, haven't you come across people who after taking an action do not own up completely, and justify, "It wasn't me, it just happened!"? I wonder, what the plight of law and order would be if we could simply walk away after committing a systemically defined sin.

The study of psychology starting roughly in the second half of the 20th century presents experimental evidence for what we think of as the self, the conscious me, the CEO who we consider to be in the driver's seat, may not be running as much of the show as we think it is. We are attributing more power to it than it truly deserves.

Sigmund Freud became famous for commenting that our behaviour is controlled to a significant extent by the unconscious forces, and the conscious mind isn't as much in charge as we think it is. The Freudian world introduced the id, ego, and superego, a three-part model of the mind. There was the id, which harbours dark animal impulses. There was what he called the superego which corresponds more or less to the conscious, and then in the middle was the ego, the self. And he indeed emphasized that the self isn't as in charge as it thinks it is, while still attributing some autonomy to it. The idea of the unconscious – the notion that what we say, do, and feel can spring from sources which we are not aware of, that are the choices and the qualities of our relationships and deeply innervated by our antiquities.

Hot off the press, the Freudian contribution has tended to be seen as historical, i.e., something we have passed beyond – but in large part, this is because popular culture has absorbed the most fundamental ideas of psychodynamics as a given. These ideas animate our view of who we are within our families, with our friends, and at our work. They add a dimension to our understanding of what it is to be human – an understanding that will become increasingly important as we confront a world in which artificial intelligence is presented to us and our children as a candidate for dialogue and relationship, and we are dragooned to a new rung of the ladder of reflection about what is extraordinary about being a person.

You may have heard of a set of landmark experiments known as the split-brain experiments, especially if you've taken an introductory psychology course any time. They've got a certain amount of publicity, and they're certainly memorable because of their strange results. These experiments involved people whose left and right hemispheres had been disconnected. We have a corpus callosum, a bundle of fibres that connects the two halves of the brain, but these people had their's surgically severed in most cases to control seizures, and when this procedure was first done, it seemed miraculous because it didn't have much effect on behaviour, aside from controlling the seizures, which is quite surprising. You'd think that the part connecting the two halves of the brain has a crucial role to play, who knows what'll happen if it gets cut. Well, not much noticeable happened.

But then in the 1960s, Michael Gazzaniga came up with an experimental apparatus that got split-brain patients to behave in quite strange ways. To ingest what he did, we must gather first the way the brain works. The information in the left half of the visual field enters the right hemisphere, and information in the right division of the visual field infiltrates into the left hemisphere, that's by natural selection. The scientists then flashed a word (like 'nut') in the left half of the visual field, which means that it entered the right half of the visual field of the hemisphere, i.e., the right hemisphere. And the way this could be told that it didn't get to the left hemisphere was they asked the patient what word was seen, while the patient insisted on not seeing any word.

Here's the explanation for that. In most people, the language faculties are housed in the left hemisphere, that's the half of the brain that does the talking. It was this part of the brain which was reporting that nothing was seen. But they had a procedure for determining that the word 'nut' had been soaked up into the right hemisphere of the brain, because this side is what controls the left hand, just as the right hand is governed by the left hemisphere, and they predicted that if they asked the patient to rummage through a box of miscellaneous objects, the left hand would cease upon a nut.

So even though, on being asked, the patient refused to have seen the word but there evidently is somewhere that the presence of that word registers, and then, in turn, motivates a behaviour, the seizing of the nut.

Isn't this affirmation strange when you think about it? Because ordinarily if a word enters your brain, it enters the conscious field, and if it influences you to take action, you think of yourself as deciding to do something in response to the information. You can share the information with the world, you can talk about what you've seen. In this case, that's not what's going on. The person can't talk about the information and the person seems to be not conscious. But we have to be careful because we really have no way of knowing that the right brain is not itself conscious. We know that the conscious left half of the brain didn't see the word, but there is no way for that half of the brain to know whether the right brain is actually experiencing things subjectively and the right brain can't say, so we don't really know what we don't know. Whimsical!

It is, therefore, the unconscious motivation or motivation that we're not aware of using subliminal techniques, where information is presented in a manner that it does not enter the conscious mind, but still does influence behaviour. Typically, in advertisements, the information is flashed so briefly on a screen that the person is not aware of having seen it, but it does influence behaviour to a degree.

Chapter 11

Human Mind – The Storyteller

Humans cotton to have a story about why they do what they do, birthing false stories at times. Since the left brain is responsible for telling stories to the world and generating the language while focusing on the overall plotline with embellishments, it is capable of, apparently, buying into massive fabrications. It's worth scrutinizing a little more, what kinds of stories as anatomically normal people, we talk about ourselves, and how true they are, or are not.

For example, if you as a shopper are unconsciously drawn to colour pencils that happen to sit on a part of the shelf that somehow appeals to you, and you are asked why you prefer that product, you come up with the claim that it has some special attribute that other products don't have, when in fact all the products on the shelf have exactly the same properties. And you seem to believe this when you say it. It's as if we're calculatedly programmed to convince the world that our motivations are coherent, and in the process, we talk ourselves into it. This has been wonderfully worded at length in a book by Rob Kurzban titled 'Why everyone else is a Hypocrite'. We're nice people. Why don't we, in other respects, injure our reputations? A built-in tendency to do this kind of self-promotion makes us look upstanding in public.

A renowned psychologist named Anthony Greenwald, in 1980, coined the term 'beneffectance' to describe the manner in which people naturally present themselves to other people. It's a compound word. The first half is borrowed from the word beneficial, implying our inclination to show our helpfulness to others, as in we'd be beneficial to them. The second half demonstrates our effectiveness. We flaunt ourselves to be capable, competent, and successful. For instance, if polled about their driving skills, most people will describe themselves as above average. When you do the arithmetic and analyze the results statistically, it can't be true that most people are above average. It won't be a normal distribution. If most people were above average, why would accidents cause a large number of deaths? This view of ourselves turns out to be extremely resistant to actual evidence.

We have this brilliant habit of not crediting negative outcomes to our deeds but focusing on ourselves when the outcomes are positive, not just in an individual context, but in a team context too when we assess how much we contributed to a team effort. In backgammon, it's the momentous roll of the dice which explains how you lost, not you. As you peer at this game example, don't you feel like playing the 'not-self card? Because it's not you who's responsible for the result but the dice.

There's one figurative study about academicians who had co-authored papers. They were asked how much of the overall effort were they responsible for. In the average four-person composition, where papers had four co-authors, the total of credit claimed by the team was 140% when they added up the evaluations of the contributors, which can be traced back to the fact that the average person was claiming more than one-third of the outcome credit. Interestingly, this finding justifies both halves of the word 'beneffectance'. In simple words, to say you contributed a lot to a team effort is to say you're effective and capable. It's also to boast you were helpful to your teammates.

Studies show that we remember the positive events in greater detail than the ones that reflect unfavourably on us. It doesn't mean we don't have any negative memories. There are explicitly some instances that unfold so disastrously that you need to remember them in order to not repeat the mistake else eraser is coveted to be our confessor, our absolver, and our time machine. Funny but heart-sickening enough, when it comes to other people, this asymmetry doesn't hold. Our capacity to remember events that reflect unfavourably on other people, in just as detailed of the genre as we remember the events that reflect favourably, stands true to itself. An example of deep-seated self-serving bias could be, the tendency to hold ourselves accountable for constructive outcomes, say that was due to our skill or hard work, whereas with the negative outcomes, we may blame unclear instructions or the fact that we were overworked or had insufficient time to execute. Where else do you observe this better than at workplace drama theatre?

In 1989, the anthropologist Jerome Barkow wrote that it can be possibly argued for the primary evolutionary function of the self to be the organ of impression management rather than, as our folk psychology would have it, a decision-maker. It blatantly projects that what we think of as the executive self was in fact educated by natural selection to be a propaganda machine.

Just visualize this situation for a moment, if a young man you meet at a networking event tells you, "I'm going to get a beer", you look at him as somebody you can do business with, someone you'd be willing to have as an acquaintance, as an ally, or as a collaborator. That's because he seems to have his act together, whereas if he had said, "You know, I'm a little weird, I do stuff, I don't know why. I get up and just walk places, even when I cannot make sense out of it. I might do any likely thing on any likely day." You are definitely not going to want that person to be on your team. This intuition about the CEO self is what's called an adaptation in biology and practically reaches the same view that the Buddha reached about 2500 years ago, preaching that the two aspects that are most deeply embedded in our intuitive notion of the self, are probably illusions as the self doesn't persist coherently through time.

Chapter 12

The Modular Mind

As with the flat and lean organizational models gaining the acclaim of present-day corporates, the modular mind view suggests that instead of one CEO, different modules seize control to get to be in charge at a given moment. There is no single department head to which they are reporting, it is free for, self-organizing system.

The specific built-in functional mechanisms in our brain are obtrusively complex and this can be supported by artificial intelligence; because AI has been in learning since the late '50s and '60s which depicts how hard it is to transfer into machines the simplest of functions that we take for granted, like the mental functions that are thought to be relatively straight forward, says facial recognition, and we don't spend a lot of time puzzling over how we manage to recognize people's faces. It seems to just happen automatically, but artificial intelligence professionals had found that to get a computer to do something like that, you need to build highly complex specialized software. The evolutionary psychologists seem to be singing the same song. As the brain has evolved over time, a lot of specific equipment has been added by natural selection, the metaphor used for this is the Swiss Army Knife.

Like a Swiss army knife has distinct blades for multifarious functions, modules have been anthologized in the human mind to perform different tasks, and to that extent, the metaphor is valid, but the metaphor has benefits as well as detriments, as there are angles in which modules don't resemble the blades of a Swiss army knife. Each blade of the knife occupies a discrete part of space. It's well defined whereas, modules are not so localized. The second sense in which modules are not like the blades on a Swiss army knife is that they're not communicating with each other whereas modules are going to have to do a certain amount of interaction and communication. The third differing sense is that the blades are all just tools. If there's no user, there's no person who decides how they're going to be used, they merely sit there and don't do anything, which isn't the case with command modules. They take turns to run the show, changing our behavioural and mental disposition in subtle steps.

What determines which module will be in charge at any given time? Easy, whichever module is most highly activated by information in the environment, will tend to become dominant for that spell of time. Suppose a goon is running toward you waving a machete saying, "I'm going to kill you", then the self-protection module would kick in and you'd start running away and screaming for help.

The other major theme in that discourse of the Buddha

was that if we boast we have conscious control of what's going on in our mind, we are mistaken. This is explained discretely by the modular view, because our state of mind at any given time is not, generally speaking, the result of conscious choice. Rather, it's the consequence of how the environmental information comes into our minds and shifts our frame of mind at a typically unconscious level.

The notion of evolutionary modules taking chances to exert dominant influence on our thoughts and behaviours dovetails nicely with the Buddhist idea of not-self, evocating no solid self at the core that persists coherently through time and serves as a lid. This close correspondence helps explain why people who are encouraging war will continue to frame the leader in the country they want to invade as evil as possible. The 2003 Iraq war was a decent example of sustaining the enemy frame with subtler feelings of antipathy.

Chapter 13

Self Control

There are times when I, the chief, makes a decision to yield to the temptation to buy a dress or hog on a chocolate mousse, but occasionally, I refrain as it's not in my long-term interest to do it. Isn't that proof of my CEO self-drawing breath?

The CEO self assumes the rank of a conscious judge adjudicating, hearing out the two parties, deciding which one has more reason on its side and then finalizing. Which is the algorithm that evaluates the merit of reasons? What makes this process conscious? Why does this all have to transcend into consciousness? Why do we have to spend energy weighing decisions before the modules?

Take the analogy of a company and instead of two contending modules, there are two contending Executive Directors. They have very different ideas about strategies, so they go to the Managing Director and provide the reasons that they can come up with for advocating their position. It's not that the Managing Director is necessarily going to declare a winner, but rather she or he is hearing the reasons so that they'll be prepared to share the reasons with the board when the time comes. If you don't have a strong reason that can be publicized, then it isn't a skilled job done.

Think of an extra-marital affair case being heard, the module advocating the affair can't come up with the truth that it wanted short term sexual gratification as that's not an acceptable answer in the society for violating a norm. This elucidates why these reasons would be rehearsed consciously. If the utility of the reasons is to be presented to others in the event that we have to share reasons, then it makes sense for the conscious mind to be communicating with other people.

In theory, there could be two separate perspectives in which reason matters. First of all, you would expect the brain to be mapped out such that it pays attention when there are good grounds for something not being in your long-term self-interest. Furthermore, to the extent that the inducement you would give people to justify something controversial you've done is not going to fly, is not going to be accepted, it needs a revisit.

Chapter 14

Mindfulness

A term that has swiped us all in addition to the complexity of our lives is 'mindfulness meditation'. Does it not confuse you at times - should you be mindful, or should you simply meditate, or do both? Well, it consists of observing anything and everything in your realm of experience, your mind, your feelings, sounds you hear, or things you see in everyday life. The clue here is - it involves observing these things in a somewhat unusual way. And second, it is controlling your thinking. For instance, you might be sitting comfortably in your chair thinking "I'm going to screw up that book launch presentation on Monday." Or you may be doing a counter-narrative and calming down saying, "Well, I'll be fine because there's nobody in the audience who really matters that much or is a close associate." But either way, anxiety is controlling what you think about, which is ironic. You've got a feeling that you really don't approve of what you don't like, and yet, you're letting it control your thoughts, your feelings, and your actions in turn. If it were to be under the shade of mindfulness meditation, you would observe a feeling without like or dislike, without judging. You'd observe it objectively. And as a result, it won't control your thoughts.

From the natural selection's point of view, it is an unnatural act, violating natural selection's agenda. Evolutionary psychology suggests that the basic biological and psychological needs are the centrally governing molecules of your life. Everything you see about the world should be focused through this lens, and that's what defines the validity of what you're paying attention to.

Mindfulness is the attention that functions in an atmosphere of detachment. It operates independently of all ulterior aims and motives, aspiring towards pure objectivity, an awareness which mirrors the nature of objects exactly as they are, without adding to them, without subtracting from them, without multiplying or dividing them, without elaborating upon them, without interpreting them through the screens of subjective evaluation and commentary.

There are three kinds of connections between mindfulness meditation and the modular view of the mind. First, the default mode network that mindfulness meditation (or any other kind of meditation for that matter) quietens, can be viewed as different modules vying for your attention. Second, by being mindful of our feelings, we principally can determine which modules are and are not allowed to take over the mind. And then third, exercising mindfulness can affect the long-term dominion of various functional modules, draining power from some and empowering others.

The singular idea is that the mind as it ordinarily works

and is designed to work in terms of the faculty of attention is not a reliable instrument of perception and thought.

Doesn't mindfulness, which is known for being gentle and implicatively soft, radical disorientation then? And what of equanimity that brushes the idea of moving beyond mindfulness and being in an even-minded mental state or dispositional tendency towards all experiences or objects?

Remember clinging and craving from the second noble truth – the cause of our pain and suffering? Clinging can also be construed as sustenance or fuel. In essence, you're fueling that fire every time you act on craving. Every time you are prompted to not get out of bed in the morning so you can escape the workout, you are enslaving yourself. Every time you crave a loaf of white bread while on a keto diet where you are to watch your carb intake and you end up cheating, you are setting yourself up for digression from your goal. Every time you wish to binge-watch a Netflix series when you should be preparing for the ongoing exam, you are subduing yourself. Every time you want an extra puff when you know you're done with your cigarette quota for the day, you are gambling with your health. Learn to just be with the craving, notice its physical sensations in the body and the mental restlessness it stimulates. If you don't act on it, it'll vanquish on its own. If you stop pouring fuel into a fire, it eventually extinguishes. If you stop feeding a stray dog, it doesn't come to your house anymore. Not the classical conditioning scene but operant conditioning is at play. But what if the dog keeps coming to your door? It can be tamed with mindfulness meditation.

You needn't worry as you are not the one thinking your thoughts. In actuality, modules generate the thoughts, but again, it might seem to you like the thoughts think themselves because the modules are outside of the realm of consciousness, so the thoughts seem to enter the consciousness of their own accord. The crisp impetus of meditation is to let your thoughts drift by like the clouds in the sky.

Chapter 15

Emptiness or Fullness?

Out there in the world, people are emptier than they seem. This might not sound upbeat though. I've never seen a living creature burst into a room saying, "I'm so happy, I finally grasped the head and tail of emptiness." The realization of this truth is momentary, at least that's how I feel.

The concept of emptiness is the most basic distinction that scholars make between the kinds of Buddhism - Theravada, and Mahayana. As a philosophical doctrine, the idea of emptiness was developed within the Mahayana tradition. However, as a meditative experience, it's common to both. Well, what is the experience of emptiness like? Don't mix it with weightlessness – that feeling in the stomach you have when swinging down from the top of a giant wheel.

The Samadhiraja Sutra quotes in this regard – 'Know all things to be like this: a mirage, a cloud castle, a dream, an apparition.' Basically, to say, nothing is real. A clinical condition called Capgras delusion aptly sheds light on the emptiness. It is a serious cognitive disorder where when people look at someone, often a loved one or a close friend, they become convinced that the person is an imposter. They don't deny that the person on the outside looks exactly like say, their sister. But they are convinced it's not their sister, on the inside, so to speak. She has the visual qualities of their sister but lacks what is the essence of sister. Anatomically, this is because there has been a disruption between the part of the brain that processes emotions and the part that does the visual processing.

Paul Bloom, who is a celebrated psychologist talks about essence from a non-Buddhist point of view. He comments that people, by nature, are essentialists. He means that it's part of our nature to see things as having an interior essence, an interior nature that we can't see but we can sense and have the intuitive idea that it's really that essence that gives them their identity. In his book 'How Pleasure Works', he writes that essence is what we attribute to living and non-living things, for instance, when people see a pine tree, there is, however subtle, a perception of the essence of the pine tree, of pine tree-ness. Generic things come with stories and those stories do inform our perception of the essence. So maybe you've got a bottle of Louis XIII cognac marketed by Remy Martin as 'one century in a bottle. Being the rarest and the most prestigious cognac in the world using high-quality Eaux-de-vie with a unique decanter shape bottle discovered at the battle of Jarnac, you cap it as astronomically valuable.

In sum, we have these interpretations and narratives of things, the conceptions of where they fit in our life story, and that shapes our feelings about them and perception of their essence, which ideally gives a touch of wholeness. It is undeniable that the stronger the feeling, the stronger is the sense of essence. Then as a formalist, won't it be a sound deal to re-term the experience as fullness rather than emptiness?

Chapter 16

True Enlightenment

Dharma (in Sanskrit) or dhamma (in Pali) is a rich word with an array of meanings. The household meaning of dharma can be established in the Buddha's teachings and by extension, in the path that the Buddha flashed for us to tread. It refers to the truth about the way the universe is structured or about the natural and moral law that structures the universe. You can rephrase that dharma means both, the truth about the way things are, and the truth about the way we ought to live in acknowledgement of the way things are. So, dharma, in the second connotation, in a cellular sense, is the unseen order. The quest in our lives, the real struggle, the goal that remains unattained, whether we confess or not, is about how to harmoniously adjust ourselves to the unseen order, and thereby realize our supreme good, which is Nirvana.

A Buddhist philosopher from the seventh century, Chandrakirti, highlighted once, 'what to a human being is water might be perceived by a certain deity as nectar or might be perceived by a hungry ghost as blood, and it would taste accordingly to those three beings.' The message is lucid, the meaning of something, the identity of something, the essence of something depends on the particular perspective of the kind of being it is.

Reconnecting to our starter, the William James quote – "the animating essence of religion is the belief that there is an unseen order and that our supreme good lies in harmoniously adjusting ourselves to that order", Buddhism ideates that the truth about the world is generally camouflaged, and if we discover it, and mellifluously align ourselves with the truth, then we will realize our supreme good. The applicative supreme good here for us is living a happy and fulfilled life, as simple as that. When you look at the order that is asserted, it does have that inspiration and potency. The gremlin and the angel, both lie within your benign self. The people who are adhering to religion in the plan is what gives their lives a meaning and complementary moral orientation, thus inspiring a very powerful commitment to this religious worldview.

Spiritually, enlightenment aligns the truth about the world, the moral truth, our fulfilment, and the end of our suffering. So, it's really kind of the trifecta, something worth marvelling at. I would say that even though Buddhism talks about an order as a divinely imparted plan that inspires awe and commitment, nonetheless, there is suffering and unsatisfactoriness. However, you can be saved by virtual contact with a higher power, not a deity but a higher form of awareness, much purer than was previously available. That's a wondrous scenario to contemplate. It insinuates a view of our evolutionary history that has a mythic quality because as far as we can tell, consciousness can only be created on this planet through natural selection. But we've also seen that natural selection, in creating consciousness tends to warp it. These twists and turns lead to various distortions that we encounter day in and day out, in perception, in cognition, and forsooth, in moral judgement. How about thinking this way - may be natural selection created consciousness and buckled it in the first place? It is upon us as self-reflective beings to figure things out and rid ourselves of these distortions imposed on the consciousness by the creator.

As you begin your journey of awareness, you'll find more continuity between you and the world, where there previously used to be fragmentation, you would now apprehend a tremendous unity, this is literally the order which had been concealed from us by the exuberantly material lifestyle. What are you picturizing at this moment? Yourself in a heave-like abode, peaceful and ethereal, out of this crazy daily bustle, severed of all relationships, akin a free soul? That is unrealistic, right? Stop daydreaming. Am I not aware of the roles and responsibilities you hold in your terrestrial life, the hopes, and ambitions you have on the personal and professional front? Of course, I am, because I am one of you with a spark to grow – a globizen, a daughter, a sister, a friend, an entrepreneur, yet to be a wife and mother. All I intend to convey is you don't have to leave this worldly setting; you can lead the usual life and still simulate Nirvana – it's just a frame of mind. Those moments during meditation when you feel you're really in touch with the real truth, you're one with the divine, and that your perception is no longer distorted by the normal distortion, inspire commitment to the practice, which is slightly comparable in its strength to the commitment that is inspired in other religions by their version of a connection with a higher power to cure the fundamental awareness in the human condition.

For those of us not looking for a substitute and have got our religion in a traditional sense, naturalistic Buddhism perfectly works like a supplement, the practice of meditation and the basic philosophy accompanying it is compatible with varicoloured religious traditions. There's a synergy between it and the major religious traditions. All of these traditions have themes and precepts that resonate with the worldview we've been describing so far. You may call it a spiritual worldview or merely a therapeutic perspective.

Glancing at the human condition from the standpoint of modern psychology, evolutionary psychology in the spotlight, and analyzing the way our evolutionary history has afflicted us with perceptual distortions, moral biases, dissatisfaction, and out and out suffering, if we ask for a world view which addresses this problem, we'd be led into a myriad of world views, religions, and therapeutic traditions that do it effectively, but a naturalistic world view that is honestly and unflinchingly on point, in my heartfelt nomination, is the one we've been chewing over.

In the 1930s, ten eighty-thousand-year-old skulls were found in Skhul Cave, at the foot of Mount Carmel in Israel. In physical attributes including shape, size, and colour, they closely resemble the skulls of Homo sapiens. A similar skull, over ninety thousand years old, was also found in a cave at Qafzeh, in Israel. That the braincases of these ancient hominids were the same as ours does not, of course, necessarily mean that their intelligence was the same as ours – although they were capable of making excellent stone tools. We now jump straight to France, to the Chevaux cave, where wall paintings of animals extant in Europe at that time are handsomely depicted and have been dated at more than thirty thousand years old. Fifteen thousand years later, in the caves at Le Portel and Lascaux, our ancestors were making magnificent polychrome paintings of animals. Their stone tools developed some five thousand years earlier, are comparable in technique and beauty to the much more recent tools of pre-Columbian America. Can anyone doubt that these Cro-Magnons, if magically brought into our present-day culture, could have learned to read, and write, to meditate, to philosophize, to do math at a high level, to learn aerodynamics and material science?

Laconically, as the human mind continues to evolve in a changing social and environmental setting, the exploration for what it takes to exist in equilibrium with the unseen order will go on, it's like that chain reaction in a nuclear reactor. But it shouldn't hold us from being the happiest version of ourselves at the present date. Yes, it is possible. I invite you to wholeheartedly embark on this journey of fulfilment, whatever stage of life you're at, whichever is your geographical location, gender, professional affiliation, caste, colour, age, economic status, etc. Let nothing deter you because you're enough, all the tools and support you need on the way is within you. You deserve to lead a life of spiritual glory!

Suggested Reads & References

1. Why Buddhism is True by Robert Wright

2. The Origin of Species by Charles Darwin

3. The Foundations of Buddhism by Ruper Gethin

4. How Pleasure Works by Paul Bloom

5. Why Everyone Else is a Hypocrite by Rob Kurzban

6. Be Here Now by Ram Dass

7. Mindfulness by Joseph Goldstein

8. Humans Are Underrated by Geoffrey Colvin

9. The Greatest Inventions of the Past 2000 Years by John Brockman

10. The Moral Animal by Robert Wright

Credits

Cover page image:

https://www.freepik.com/free-vector/watercolor-vesak-day-illustration_12811913.htm#query=buddha+purnima++vesak&position=10

https://www.freepik.com/free-vector/water-color-vesak-day-illustration_12805370.htm#page=1&query=buddha&position=34

Glyph Image:

https://commons.wikimedia.org/wiki/File:Threejewels.svg

www.ingramcontent.com/pod-product-compliance
Lightning Source LLC
LaVergne TN
LVHW091606170726
843492LV00007B/2284